Discipleship

Biblical, Contemporary and Personal Reflections on Christian Discipleship

ALEX JACOB

ENDORSEMENTS

This book comes out of experience, with real churches and the people who make them up. Alex Jacob presents Christian discipleship, not as a formula or a fix, but as a steady, thoughtful commitment to live a Jesus-shaped life in our own corner of God's world. The writing is clear and honest, and the chapters are helpfully bite-sized. Here is a wise author to learn with, and a resource that is well worth using.

John Proctor. Director of New Testament Studies, Westminster College Cambridge (1986-2014) and United Reformed Church General Secretary (2014-2020).

This is a thoughtful book on discipleship for thoughtful people! I gladly recommend it to those who are leading other people on the discipleship journey and any individuals who are serious about growing as disciples of Jesus.

Stephen Gaukroger. Director of Clarion Trust International and President of the Baptist Union of Great Britian (1994-1995).

In Discipleship, Alex Jacob brings the richness of Biblical insight and the logic of a sequence of steps to nourish and nurture readers' Christian life. As a companion with him on the Way, I know Alex writes of what he lives. I think many will find encouragement here, as they journey through the steps, and on reaching the tenth, are inspired to keep on going.

Nigel Uden. Minister of Fulbourn and Downing Place Cambridge and Moderator of United Reformed Church General Assembly (2018-2020).

Having had the privilege of Alex's support in my ministry for over ten years, his heart for Jesus and discipleship of His followers is unquestionable. This is obvious throughout the ten-step study. I love that this study is Jesus focused and continuously focused on Scripture. The points to consider after each chapter are inspired. An all-round excellent book that will be a useful tool for every believer in Jesus.

Chris Kemshell. Pastor of Linton Free Church and author of 'Cancer and the Cross' (2023).

Copyright © 2024 Alex Jacob

All rights reserved.

The right of Alex Jacob
to be identified as the author of this work
has been asserted by him in accordance with
the Copyright, Designs and Patents Act 1988.
All rights reserved.

No part of this publication may be reproduced or transmitted in any form of by any means, electronic or mechanical, including photocopy, recording or any information storage and retrieval system, without prior permission in writing from the publisher.

First published in Great Britain by
Christian Publications International
("CPI") an imprint of Inspiration – Assurance Publications
PO Box 212 Saffron Walden CB10 2UU UK

Unless otherwise stated, Scripture quotations are taken from the
Holy Bible, New International Version ®
Copyright © 1984 by International Bible Society.
Used by permission of Hodder & Stoughton Publishers, a member of the Hodder Headline Group. All rights reserved. 'NIV' is a registered trademark of International Bible Society. UK trademark number 1448790. All rights reserved.

www.christian publications-int.com

Readers are encouraged to compare assertions in all CPI books with the clear witness of Scripture. CPI offers this book as a contribution towards continuing study of the inspired Word of God, which the publisher considers to be the final 'court of appeal' in matters of faith and doctrine.

ISBN 978-1-913741-17-4

Printed in Great Britain by Imprint Digital, Exeter
and worldwide by Ingram-Spark

CONTENTS

7 Dedication
9 Introduction
15 The Biblical Context of Discipleship
21 Oh, No. Not More Lists!
The Top Ten Steps for Faithful and Effective Christian Discipleship

STEP ONE 23
Sharing the Hope

30 **STEP TWO**
Learning to Give

STEP THREE 33
Growing in Prayer

41 **STEP FOUR**
Willing to Forgive

STEP FIVE 49
Willing to Go

55 **STEP SIX**
Focusing on Worship

STEP SEVEN 61
Committing to Study

67 **STEP EIGHT**
Recognising your Gifting

STEP NINE 73
Seeking the Kingdom

79 **STEP TEN**
Keeping on Going

85 Bibliography
87 Biblical References
89 Books by Alex Jacob
90 Contact Information

DEDICATION

I dedicate this book to all
who are seeking to live out **John 15:8**

This is to my Father's glory, that you bear much fruit, showing yourselves to be my disciples.

INTRODUCTION

"When Christ calls a man, he bids him come and die." So wrote Dietrich Bonhoeffer(1906-1945) in his seminal book *The Cost of Discipleship*.[1] Bonhoeffer in his writing, living and martyrdom gives some special insights into Christian discipleship.[2] His emphasis on the cost of discipleship reminds us that the shape of true discipleship is often forged by opposition, persecution and martyrdom.

This was certainly the case in the early Church and the reality of martyrdom shaped how the Church related to the wider culture. The first martyr of the Church is Stephen (Acts 7:54-60), following this, persecution and martyrdom continued in a range of places throughout the history of the Church and remains the reality faced by many Christian disciples today. It is worth noting that the New Testament Greek word for bearing witness or giving testimony is *'martureo'*, which can also be translated as 'to martyr.' This word is used 79 times in the New Testament.

Bonhoeffer, for me along with several other key Christians throughout history, is a prime example and an inspiration to take seriously my calling as a disciple of Jesus. Yet, when I read his writings and reflect on his life, I feel he was playing in and gracing the 'premier league' while I am occasionally selected to make up the numbers when my local Sunday league football team is desperately short of players. I have not written this book because I see myself as any kind of expert on discipleship, far from it. I have written this because I want to do better myself and I want to help resource others to do better as well.

This sense of somehow not living out fully the call to be a disciple of Jesus is something which is experienced by most Christians I know.

---

1. Dietrich Bonhoeffer, *The Cost of Discipleship*, First published in German (1937) and first English edition published in 1951. See bibliography for details.
2. A helpful introduction to the life and ministry of Dietrich Bonhoeffer is given by Mary Bosanquet in her book, *Bonhoeffer-True Patriot*, Mowbrays, 1968.

This reality is reflected in much teaching and writing about parts of the contemporary Church. A good example of this is in the writing of David Watson (1933-1984), who taught that, if we were willing to learn the meaning of true discipleship and actually to become disciples, the Church in the West would be transformed and the resultant impact on society would be staggering. David Watson wrote and taught widely about ministry and discipleship within a contemporary setting. His key book in this regard is entitled simply *Discipleship*.[3]

In attempting to write about Christian discipleship I am not seeking to stir up guilt in anyone, for guilt is seldom a good motivating tool; yet I have found that a Holy Spirit inspired discontentment can be a helpful first step for spiritual questioning and growth.

Every piece of writing has a context, and this book is no different. The context for writing this is that I have been a Christian for nearly fifty years and, for forty of them, I have been working mainly in the UK as an ordained Church Minister. I became a Christian as a young teenager. As with any journey of faith, there are many 'moving parts' but I remember being particularly challenged and encouraged by Jesus' words of invitation: "*A thief comes only to rob, kill, and destroy. I came so that everyone would have life, and have it in its fullest*" (John 10:10).[4] At first these words of Jesus may seem to contradict completely the words of Dietrich Bonhoeffer: "*When Christ (Jesus) calls a man, he bids him come to die.*" However, I understand that there is no contradiction, but rather we discover two sides of the one coin of discipleship. Discipleship is rooted both in the cross of Christ and in Christ's resurrection. Discipleship is embedded in dying to yourself and seeking to live in the fulness of the Holy Spirit. Discipleship is at its very core a living out of the counter-cultural Christian doctrine of human nature as transformed and restored in Christ.

---

3. David Watson, *Discipleship*, Hodder & Stoughton, 1981. See also by David Watson, *Is Anyone There?* Hodder Paperbacks, 1983.

4. This quotation is taken from the Contemporary English Version. However, most other Bible quotations are taken from the New International Version (Anglicised edition, revised and updated 2011). When other versions are used rather than the New International Version this will be noted in the text.

Currently I am working with groups of United Reformed Churches (some of which are linked within ecumenical partnerships), most of which have experienced some significant decline -both in numbers of members, community support and in missional effectiveness. My hope is to be part of a team that helps these Churches discern how they can work together with a greater missional focus and find ways for their life and witness to be resourced and renewed for the next generation.

In this work there is an emphasis on 'whole-life' discipleship and new models of Church leadership. To aid this, the United Reformed Church has produced a discipleship development programme known as 'Stepwise'.[5] This interactive discussion-focused approach begins with the 'Faith-filled Life' course which has been designed for people of all ages and stages of Christian discipleship. The focus of this is that you cannot truly grow as a disciple without a context for mission. The most immediate context for mission is our day-to-day lives, and whatever we are doing we are called to follow Jesus and to share good news. In this evolving context many questions are being posed and explored, for example questions such as:

"Is it possible to change the focus of a Church from what happens only on a Sunday to how the Church equips people for living as disciples every day of the week and in every context?"

"How can we build discipleship-making communities within a post-modern secular context?"

"How can we best work in partnership with others?"

"Imagine what could happen, if every Church member looked around at the people, they spend time with and asked God: 'How do you want me to be good news to these people today'?"

"How can we creatively deploy the assets of the Church so that the beauty and truth of the Gospel connects with modern life and culture?"

---

5. You can access the Stepwise hub via any web browser. Stepwise resources are contained within the United Reformed Church online learning hub.

"Is it possible to move from a 'maintenance' view of ministry to a 'mission' focused view of ministry?"

"How can we resource and commit to helping each other grow as disciples?"

These types of question lead us to some serious reflection and hopefully to a commitment to exploring and embracing "whole-life discipleship and mission". What this really means in practice will clearly vary in differing contexts, as well as for each of us as part of local Church communities and as individual disciples.

Thinking and teaching about such questions is a huge project and some helpful resources are available. In terms of books, I would like to flag up three in this introduction which I have found useful.

Firstly, the Grove Leadership Booklet (L7): *Leading a Whole-Life Disciplemaking Church*.[6] This booklet by Tracy Cotterell and Neil Hudson is a great starting point for any Church leader who wants to explore discipleship and mission.

Secondly, the book *Apologetic Preaching – Proclaiming Christ to a Postmodern World*.[7] This book by Craig A. Loscalzo provides a firm foundation for all those seeking to preach, teach and share the Gospel within a contemporary context.

Thirdly, the book *Biblical Critical Theory – How the Bible's Unfolding Story Makes Sense of Modern Life and Culture*.[8] This book by Christopher Watkin is a magnificent and comprehensive work bringing the Scriptures into a transformative, subversive and illuminating conversation with our modern world and its controlling cultures. Within this book Watkin shares some very powerful insights relating to the challenges Christian disciples face today. For example, Watkin writes: "*It is emblematic of the radical nature of orthodoxy in the last days: there is nothing quite so*

---

6. Published by Grove Books Limited, Ridley Hall, Cambridge, 2012.
7. Published by Inter-Varsity Press, 2000.
8. Published by Zondervan Academic, 2023.

radically subversive today as sound doctrine and godly living."[9] And later he writes: *"To live as a Christian in the last days of late modernity is to live amidst a hegemonic cultural heresy, neither utterly alien to the faith nor a faithful continuation of it. The situation demands of Christians a subtlety and discernment perhaps unprecedented in the history of the church."*[10]

In what follows in this book on discipleship I will not attempt to answer directly any of the questions listed in this introduction, but these questions do provide the context for much of what I seek to share. My focus will be on personal discipleship. Yet it is clear that our discipleship is always within a wider community context. As the early Church theologian, apologist and author Tertullian (160-240) taught: *"No Christian is a Christian alone."*

Back in 2018, I wrote a brief commentary on Luke's Gospel,[11] and this was written primarily to help new Jewish Believers in Jesus (Messianic Jews). I was at this time working with a mission agency focusing on mission within the context of Jewish-Christian relations. The first paragraph of this book reads: *"Becoming a disciple of Jesus (Yeshua) is the most important and transformative decision anyone can make. Following this decision, my prayer is that everyone will continue to grow in faith, love and understanding, and that above all our relationships with Jesus will deepen."*

This new book on discipleship is my attempt to take the next step and help resource growth for disciples of Jesus, regardless of our backgrounds, identities, Church traditions, ages etc. I will try and do this by firstly placing discipleship into its prime Biblical context and then by focusing on ten practical steps for faithful and effective discipleship today.

After each of the Ten Steps there are some points to consider. Hopefully such points may help us all in our personal reflections and will also be a catalyst for further study, prayerful reflection and group discussions.

---

9. Christopher Watkin, *Biblical Critical Theory*, Zondervan Academic, 2023, p.482.
10. See above footnote 9, p.526.
11. Alex Jacob, *100 Days with Luke*, Christian Publications International, 2018.

THE BIBLICAL CONTEXT OF DISCIPLESHIP

Even an initial superficial reading of the Gospel accounts and the Book of Acts would give the impression that discipleship is a key Scriptural theme. The word disciple or disciples appears 71 times in Matthew's account, 46 times in Mark, 35 times in Luke, 66 times in John and 26 times in Acts.

The word disciple (*'mathetes'* in New Testament Greek) is primarily used for the relational link between Jesus and His immediate circle of followers. Other New Testament words and descriptions, such as those belonging to The Way, those who call upon the name of the LORD, brothers, saints, friends, Nazarenes[1] and believers are also used. And while a case can be made that the word believers is the first collective word to be used for the embryonic community gathering around Jesus, it is very compelling to see the word disciple as the word which most widely and strongly affirms and celebrates the identity of those committed personally and collectively to Jesus.

I believe that, based on a careful study of the Gospels and the missional work of the early Church the best way to sum up the ministry of Jesus is to see that His message is the message of the Kingdom,[2] and the method for responding fully to His message is to be found in becoming a faithful disciple of Jesus.

---
1. The description 'Nazarenes' reflects a particular Jewish way of designating Jesus' disciples as those who follow the Nazarene (the man from Nazareth). See Acts 24:5. The term was widely used in a Syrian Christian context and by Armenians and later by many Arab groups.
2. For a helpful overview of the Biblical theology of the kingdom see the book by Michael J. Vlach – *He will Reign Forever– A Biblical Theology of the Kingdom of God*, Lampion House, 2017.

Jesus began His ministry by proclaiming the kingdom, the kingdom of God which is near and invites a radical change of hearts and lives (Mark 1:15). The parables Jesus taught are 'kingdom parables' (Matthew 13:44) showing the values and reality embedded in God's rule. The healing ministry of Jesus demonstrates God's kingdom power and promises. The prayer life and teaching of Jesus is kingdom-focused (Matthew 6:10). His teaching is kingdom-focused (Matthew 5:3 and 5:10) and His final commission to His disciples is to go and make known the kingdom by making, baptising and teaching new disciples (Matthew 28:19-20).

Kingdom and discipleship are intrinsically linked. Kingdom is the message; discipleship is the method!

The word disciple refers not just to the initial Twelve called by Jesus in the Gospel accounts but to all who, down through the generations, have responded to the call by Jesus to discipleship. This call is always a call to Jesus, a call to follow and trust Him as Saviour and LORD. Clearly there was to some degree a specific and special relationship between Jesus and the Twelve, yet nevertheless the privilege and responsibility of discipleship is not limited to these first Twelve.

It is also worth noting while the word disciple is not used beyond the Gospels and the Book of Acts, it is however the term which best affirms and celebrates the teacher-student relationship and is, I believe, probably the most widely used descriptive term today by Christians who are seeking to self-identify and explain their personal and collective commitment to Jesus as Saviour and LORD.

While there are some key activities and commitments shared by all disciples of Jesus (hopefully these are addressed in part within the Ten Steps which will be my focus in what follows in this book) there is however no 'one-size-fits-all' model of discipleship, but rather a huge and rich diversity of ways in which faithful and authentic discipleship is lived out. The true source for this diversity, this faithfulness and this authenticity, is found in the teaching of Paul, who in 1 Corinthians 10:31 writes: *"So whether you eat or drink or whatever you do, do it all for the glory of God."*

The understanding of being a disciple, however, is not limited simply within a Biblical context to a relationship with Jesus. If we look back in the Biblical text, we see a number of examples of the free acceptance by a person of another as their guide, spiritual tutor and master. A good example is in the relationship between Moses and Joshua. In Exodus 33:11 Joshua is described as Moses' young assistant or servant. Joshua is clearly in a learning and serving relationship with Moses. Later in Numbers 27, the LORD instructs Moses to prepare the way for Joshua to succeed him and for Joshua to lead the Israelite community. Deuteronomy 34 also tells of the death of Moses and the emerging leadership of Joshua.

Another example is the relationship of Elijah and Elisha as recounted in 1 Kings 19 and 2 Kings 2. Also in 2 Kings 2:3(and 2 Kings 4:38) we read of the *"sons of the prophets"* (Authorised Version) who seem to establish some form of community or company of those aspiring to exercise a prophetic ministry and appear to seek out key prophets such as Elijah and Elisha in order to learn from them and to receive a blessing from them. The Hebrew indicates that the word son (*ben*) should be understood in this context as a pupil. Many commentators suggest that the term *"sons of the prophets"* (Authorised Version), *"company of the prophets"* (New International Version) or *"guild of prophets"* (Complete Jewish Bible) could be better translated as *"disciples of the prophets"*.

These examples from the Books of Moses (Torah) and the Prophets (Nevi'im) of some form of teacher-disciple relationship in the Bible remind us that the concept of discipleship which Jesus used in His teaching and wider ministry was well rooted in Jewish Biblical thought, as indeed was the concept of God's kingdom. It is not that Jesus in His ministry is inventing new concepts, for example, He is recognised as a 'Rabbi',[3] but rather He is continuing with the Biblical revelation and bringing this to fulfilment. He is taking existing Biblical concepts such as kingdom and discipleship and filling them with radical new depth and messianic meaning.

---

3. A Jewish traditional title affirming a religious teacher/leader. Jesus is addressed as Rabbi in John 1:38, 1:49, 3:2, 3:26, 6:25 and as Rabboni (the Aramaic word for Rabbi) in John 20:16.

It is also significant to note that, in post Biblical Rabbinical Jewish traditions one can continue to see the importance of discipleship. This is especially clear in Hasidic Jewish practice in which discipleship is of the utmost importance. A faithful Hasid must be a disciple of a particular Rabbi (or school of Rabbinic teaching). A faithful Hasid must not simply learn Torah from his Rabbi, but must try and imitate every aspect of his Rabbi's daily living, customs and manners.

A well-known and oft-repeated story makes this point clear: the Hasidic leader and preacher Dov Ber of Mezeritch (1704-1772) taught that he did not visit his spiritual leader to only study Torah or discuss religious theory, but to witness how he tied his shoelaces.

As a disciple of Jesus, I have no knowledge of how Jesus tied his shoelaces - I am not even sure if Jesus had shoelaces.[4] In fact, I know nothing for certain about His footwear, and, as far as I know, this area of ignorance has not hindered in any way my discipleship. Nevertheless, the wider point is compelling. Namely I want to model my life on Jesus, I want to pursue being like Jesus, I want to be obedient to His perfect will, I want to know Him and be known as fully as possible. I want the intimacy of which Jesus speaks in John 14:23: "*...If anyone loves me, they will obey me. Then my Father will love them, and we will come to them and live in them.*" (Contemporary English Version). The essence of Christian discipleship - this deep sense of imitating Jesus is taken up by Paul when he writes in 1 Corinthians 11:1: "*You must follow my example, as I follow the example of Christ.*" (Contemporary English Version).

I am clear that this close and intense learning relationship, gleaned in part from a study of Hasidic practice, gives many helpful insights into the true meaning of discipleship as taught by Jesus. For we who are disciples of Jesus are seeking not simply to learn from our risen LORD, but also to do as He would do and to become more like Him as we are continually renewed and restored by His Spirit.

The purpose of this effort, this pursuit, this imitation, this journey of

---

4. The only text I could find which may help to shed some light upon my ignorance is John 1:27.

discipleship, is summed up beautifully by Jesus in His words as recalled in John 15:8: *"This is to my Father's glory, that you bear much fruit, showing yourselves to be my disciples."*

How we work towards this purpose, and the steps we need to take is of pressing importance, and this is where we turn our attention in the following sections of this book.

OH NO. NOT MORE LISTS!
The Top Ten Steps for Faithful and Effective Christian Discipleship

When Christians preach (or write books) along the lines of "Three ways to grow your prayer life," or "Twenty ways to witness effectively to your local community," along with "Six guaranteed ways to enrich your Church worship", they provoke in me a growing aversion. Such lists are endless, and contemporary Christian media are full of them.

I think my aversion springs from my tendency to see that such lists and titles have more to do with contemporary marketing and presentation techniques than with a serious engagement with the Bible and with real life. Also, this type of approach smacks of 'self-help' mantras rather than of an honest and authentic engagement with the work of the Holy Spirit. So please forgive me and my related blatant hypocrisy as I offer the Top Ten steps for faithful and effective discipleship!

All I can offer in my somewhat flimsy defence is that this list is based upon many conversations with a wide range of Christians whom I deeply respect. Also, these steps have been 'road-tested' over many years and in many contexts. Moreover, please don't see my list as in anyway 'definitive'. It is simply offered in order to give structure to my teaching on discipleship. I hope what follows is not seen in anyway as manipulative or programmatic, but rather as useful tools to help us all explore the depths of discipleship and to assist us discern how to grow as disciples of Jesus.

So here goes; the list is as follows:

Step One- Sharing the Hope

Step Two- Learning to Give

Step Three- Growing in Prayer

Step Four- Willing to Forgive

Step Five- Willing to Go

Step Six - Focusing on Worship

Step Seven- Committing to Study

Step Eight- Recognising your Giftings

Step Nine- Seeking the Kingdom

Step Ten- Keeping on Going

It is to the first step we now turn.

Points to consider

- What changes would you want to make to my Top Ten list? What is missing?

- Write out your Top Ten list.

- How do you think your list may change (or has changed) over the years? If changes have occurred, why do you think this has been the case?

STEP ONE
Sharing the Hope

STEP ONE - SHARING THE HOPE

This first step of authentic Christian discipleship is rooted in the conviction that the Gospel is 'good news' for all people, in all places and at all times. Whoever becomes a disciple of Jesus is living out the highest calling possible. Step one is therefore a commitment to sharing this conviction and the hope we have. It is being obedient to the instruction given in 1 Peter 3:15: *"...in your hearts revere Christ as Lord. Always be prepared to give an answer to everyone who asks you to give the reason for the hope you have. But do this with gentleness and respect."*

The text of 1 Peter affirms the inclusive and wide-ranging responsibility of sharing the hope we have. We are not instructed simply to give an answer to a few people, perhaps those we know well, or feel an affection towards, but rather to everyone. This inclusivity reflects the very heart of the mission of God, as declared in John 3:16: *"For God so loved the world that he gave his one and only Son, that whoever believes in him shall not perish but have eternal life."*[1] We are all included, for all of us are sinners (Romans 3:23), and sin leads to death (Romans 6:23). All have rebelled against God; we are all equal. Equal in deserving the judgement of God resulting from our sin.

We are also equal as we all need to hear and respond to the call of Jesus, the call to discipleship. 1 Timothy 2:4-6 affirms that this call is for all, as God *"...wants all people to be saved and to come to a knowledge of the truth. For there is one God and one mediator between God and mankind, the man Christ Jesus, who gave himself as a ransom for all people."*

There are no specific qualifications required to be a disciple, no curriculum vitae need to be submitted, no references are sought. This 'open door to all' is reflected in the diverse nature of those living out the call to discipleship and following on from this the diverse membership of the Church. For example, as Revelation 7:9 reads: *"...I looked, and there before was a great multitude that no one could count, from every nation, tribe, people and language, standing before the throne and before the Lamb."*

---

1. The term *'so'* in this text means *'in this way'* and not *'how much.'*

This wonderful diversity, this inclusivity, is a gift of God - a gift in which unity without stifling uniformity is celebrated. There is a richness as each person rooted in different nations, tribes and cultural contexts brings their unique perspectives and giftings as they seek to live and serve as disciples. Yet within this diversity and inclusivity there is also an essential exclusivity. This inclusivity is therefore not entirely absolute or universal, for it is limited to those who know that they are in need of mercy and forgiveness, and following on from knowing this need, they call on the name of the Lord (Romans 10:9-13) and put their trust in Him.

This 'knowing', 'responding' and 'trusting' is the outworking of grace, and grace fosters genuine faith rooted in Jesus alone, and grace calls for and empowers true repentance. As we read in John 14:6: *"Jesus answered, 'I am the way and the truth and the life. No one comes to the Father except through me'."* A similar truth is expressed in Acts 4:12, where we read: *"Salvation is found in no one else, for there is no other name under heaven given to mankind by which we must be saved."*

This outworking of grace undermines any attempt to justify ourselves based on our performance or on any other measurement of status: it is grace that makes Christian discipleship and Christianity itself the most 'inclusive exclusivity' imaginable.

In the light of this we need to make sure that, in order to take step one in our journey we understand that no-one is beyond the hope and salvation offered in Jesus. We must learn to not make shallow judgements and to root out any prejudices or assumptions that certain types of people are beyond the redemptive reach of the LORD. We need to be open to everyone who asks. Having understood this, we must express this attitude of openness in specific actions, and in fostering key values.

Our first action in being open to everyone who asks, is to be a friend. This reminds us that we are looking to be open to form genuine relationships and to engage in authentic conversations. I think for the vast majority of us 'friendship evangelism' will be our most natural and effective way of 'sharing the hope'.

Our second action is to be patient. Most effective missional conversations and encounters are long-term investments. They are best understood as a long-term process rather than single disconnected events. With this in mind we must be patient and try to discern the LORD's perfect timing.

Our third action is to be faithful - faithful to Scripture and faithful to our experience. In this faithfulness we need to develop a clear, mature and compelling view of the Gospel message and of our own experience (testimony). In our conversations we need to avoid being side-tracked into secondary issues and rather to keep the focus upon Jesus. We are to be a signpost pointing to Jesus and not to ourselves.[2] In attempting to do this, we need to discern when questions are genuine and pressing. When this is the case, we must do all we can to answer as helpfully as we can. However, if questions are not genuine but rather are aimed to distract or trap us, don't try to answer such insincere questions with a genuine answer, but respond with a sincere question. As we read the Gospel accounts, we will discover how Jesus Himself gives us prime examples of how to engage faithfully with both genuine seekers and insincere opponents.

There is also a place for the use of logic and reason in our answering. However, in these conversations, we are not trying to impress someone with our knowledge or eloquence, nor are we seeking to win an argument, but rather to build relationships and to share the hope we have. Don't be afraid to say so if you don't know the answer to a specific question. And don't try and disguise your own doubts, questions or weaknesses[3]- be authentic to who you are.

Our fourth action is to be prayerful. We need God's power and help in sharing the hope we have. Sharing the hope and having effective missional conversations are never about selling a product, promoting an institution or trying to rearrange the mental furniture in someone's mind. It is always far greater than all of this: it is a deep transformative

---

2. This pointing away from ourselves (and to Jesus) seems to me to be the opposite of most contemporary social media agendas and profiles which seem to be focused resolutely on promoting yourself or a product. John the Baptist is a prime example of this pointing away from ourselves and directly to Jesus — see John 3:30.

3. See 2 Corinthians 12:9.

work of God. Such work must be handled with care and prayer!

The 'gold standard' in developing missional encounters is to discern and develop genuine points of contact. You may already have an excellent network of contacts via friendships, family, work colleagues, social, cultural and political activities etc. Be thankful if this is the case. If this is not the case try and develop such points of contact; and be intentional about this, both personally and through supporting the missional activities of your local Church community.

Points to consider

- What has helped you in terms of sharing the hope you have?
- How can you cultivate gentleness and respect in your engagement with those who are seeking to find out more about Jesus?
- What do you see as the biggest obstacle to those you know who are considering the claims of the Gospel and becoming a disciple of Jesus?
- Try and memorize 1 Timothy 2:4-6 and Romans 10:9-13.

STEP TWO
Learning to Give

STEP TWO - LEARNING TO GIVE

As disciples of Jesus, we are called to be 'counter cultural agents of change'. This is a huge challenge, and the context of this challenge for many of us is in terms of how we give. We come face to face with the command to give though the words of Jesus in Luke 6:30: *"Give to everyone who asks you, and if anyone takes what belongs to you, do not demand it back."* Later in the same section (6:36) of teaching Jesus calls us to: *"Be merciful, just as your Father is merciful."*

This call to giving and showing mercy flows out of love. Love is the foundation of all of Jesus' teaching and actions. This should not surprise us, for *"God is love"* (1 John 4:8). The Swiss theologian Emil Brunner (1889-1966) wrote that these words are: *"The most daring statement that has ever been made in human language."*[1]

We see and understand the nature of true love in and through Jesus, and it is love which motivates the redemptive actions of God (John 3:16).

The importance of giving is especially highlighted in a consumer society where our identity often seems to be based on what we have acquired or what we consume, while the kingdom perspective is more truly seen in how we give. This point is made powerfully by Jesus in His teaching regarding the sheep and the goats in Matthew 25:31-46.

Sometimes we may give but not love (our giving may be stirred in such cases by pride or a desire to control), but we can never love without giving. As disciples we must cultivate the art of giving generously. This involves discipline and selflessness on our part, but we freely acknowledge that such giving is always prompted and empowered by the gracious work of the Holy Spirit. Learning to give is seldom easy, but by God's grace we can move forward in this regard. Perhaps initial steps can include simple acts of kindness to those around us, acts of hospitality, an awareness of those in need and regular and sacrificial giving within our Church community. We must also learn to enjoy God's gifts we have received, for not to enjoy them would be to dishonour the

---

1. Emil Brunner, *Dogmatics*, vol 1, *The Christian Doctrine of God* (Westminster Press, 1950) p.122.

Giver. There are things a disciple must renounce, but such renunciation is never a denial of the goodness of God and the gifts of His creation.

We see many examples of this Holy Spirit inspired giving in the Church, but perhaps the most well-known example is in Acts 2:42-47. Here Luke gives a brief and compelling glimpse into the community life of the early Church, where we see generous giving embedded in deep devotion. There is a commitment to what is evidently a fourfold model of community life based upon teaching, fellowship, the breaking of bread and prayer. Within this community there is radical giving and a powerful concern for those in need.

Today as disciples, both individually and collectively as part of a Church community, we need to learn to give. We need God's help in being set free from the hold of our consumer society which endlessly stimulates our 'consumption desires'. Together we must seek to develop ways of radical giving, alongside a just sharing of resources. We must also pursue faithful and sustainable ways of creating and redistributing wealth.

> **Points to consider**
>
> - Read Proverbs 30:8-9. How can we navigate the path between poverty and riches?
> - Can you give examples of when you have been helped and encouraged by the generosity of others?
> - Is the principle of tithing helpful in shaping Christian giving today?

STEP THREE
Growing in Prayer

STEP THREE - GROWING IN PRAYER

Prayer is rooted in Christian discipleship. It is part of our on-going and intimate engagement with God - Father, Son and Holy Spirit.

For many of us, we would affirm and celebrate that our Christian life began when we prayed a prayer of simple commitment to Jesus —a prayer similar to this: *"LORD Jesus I want to know You and follow You, please forgive me for my sins and selfishness. Thank-You for dying on the cross and rising from the dead for me. Help me to give myself to You and to follow You all the days of my life. Please fill me with Your Holy Spirit and guide me always."*[1]

Sometimes this prayer would be offered to God in private or with the support of a trusted Christian. The circumstances which have led to this prayer will be far-ranging. Often the person praying this prayer will come with a tangled mass of motives and emotions. Alongside this prayer there will be many questions, yet such prayer when offered in sincerity, is always a sign of God's active grace and a demonstration of trust and obedience which flows from encountering the Gospel.

This simple prayer of commitment is part of the wider Biblical witness to prayer. Prayer in its most direct form is simply a calling (or crying) out to God.[2] The first time such a prayer is mentioned in the Biblical text is in Genesis 4:26. Later in the beginning of the Exodus account (Exodus 2:23-24) we read: *"...The Israelites groaned in their slavery and cried out, and their cry for help because of their slavery went up to God. God heard their groaning and he remembered his covenant with Abraham, with Isaac and with Jacob."* The Exodus story continues with God hearing the cries of His people and remembering His covenant promises, and this hearing and remembering are the catalyst for the Israelites' liberation from oppression in Egypt.

The Psalms also provide rich insights into the reality of prayer. The Psalms are a wonderful mix of praise and prayer - prayers which are both individual and corporate, spontaneous and liturgical and which cover a vast range of human emotions including guilt, fear, anger, joy

---

1. Prayers along these lines are sometimes known as the 'sinners' prayer'.
2. This 'calling out' can also be understood as 'to proclaim' or 'call on' the name of the LORD.

and thankfulness. Some are full of mercy while others are bitter. Some are altruistic while others appear selfish. Maybe the Psalms reflect our own prayers which can contain the good and the bad, the pure and impure. Richard Foster in his perceptive and helpful book on prayer, reflects on our mixed motives and writes: *"I have come to see that God is big enough to receive us with all our mixture. We do not have to be bright or pure, or filled with faith, or anything. That is what grace means, and not only are we saved by grace, we live by it as well. And we pray by it. Jesus reminds us that prayer is a little like children coming to their parents. Our children come to us with the craziest requests at times. Often, we are grieved by the meanness and selfishness of their requests, but we would be all the more grieved if they never came to us, even with their meanness and selfishness. We are simply glad they do come – mixed motives and all."*[3]

As we turn to the Gospel records, we see many examples of Jesus praying and encouraging and inspiring His disciples to pray as well. However, the Gospel material does not give us precise information of how and when Jesus prayed. For example, the Bible commentator Joachim Jeremias argues: *"...no day in the life of Jesus passed without the three times of prayer (morning, afternoon and evening)."*[4] While this may be true, the Gospel records are not detailed enough for us to state this with certainty. It is also interesting to note that, at one point,[5] Jesus was reproached for not praying and fasting as the disciples of John the Baptist did, but rather He enjoyed eating and drinking with tax collectors and sinners.[6] This may have caused some concern to His disciples. There remains some mystery about how and when Jesus prayed.

I think this degree of mystery is helpful, for we are not given a precise method to follow mechanically but rather we are given a person to be inspired by. A helpful illustration of this insight is shared in the biography[7]

---

3. Richard Foster, *Prayer*, Hodder and Stoughton, 1992, p.8.
4. Joachim Jeremias *The Prayers of Jesus*, SCM Press, 2012.
5. See Matthew 9:14 and Luke 5:33.
6. See Luke 5: 27-32.
7. Collier Winn, *A Burning in my Bones* – (Authorized biography of Eugene H. Peterson), Authentic Media, 2020, p31-32.

of Eugene Peterson (1932-2018), where Winn Collier writes: *"John Wright Follette, a Pentecostal leader, stayed with the Petersons for the summer when Eugene was fifteen. Follette was a Pentecostal mystic, a teacher of deep matters of the soul and life with God. In awe of Follette, Eugene told his mother that he wanted to talk to him, and she encouraged him to go out to where Follette was lying in his hammock. Eugene timidly approached and asked, "Dr. Follette, how do you pray?" The teacher didn't even open his eyes. He just grinned and grunted. "I haven't prayed in forty years!". "That stunned me," Eugene recounted decades later. "I walked off totally puzzled." Over the years, however, the shock of that moment unfolded profound wisdom –* (Eugene in reflecting on this said) *"You see, anything he had told me I would have imitated. I would have done what he said he did and thought that's what prayer is. He risked something to teach me what prayer was, and I'm glad he did. Prayer wasn't something he did – it was something he was. He lived a life of prayer. It took me about six or seven years to understand what he had done. But it was sure better than wasting time trying to imitate what he did."*

While there remains a helpful mystery about how and when Jesus prayed, we know that Jesus linked prayer to trust and obedience (Matthew 6:8). We know that He warned against vain repetition (Matthew 6:7) and public spectacles of 'piety' (Matthew 6:5). We know that He chose to teach His disciples one prayer -a prayer which is simple and brief, yet contains so much insight and meaning we can build an entire life of prayer upon it. Let's explore some key insights from this prayer which can help shape our prayer life as disciples. The prayer is set out in Matthew 6:9-13 and Luke 11:2-4.

Let's focus on the Matthew text of this prayer which is slightly more extended than Luke's. Matthew's text reads: *"This, then, is how you should pray: 'Our Father in heaven, hallowed be your name, your kingdom come, your will be done, on earth as it is in heaven. Give us today our daily bread. And forgive us our debts, as we also have forgiven our debtors. And lead us not into temptation, but deliver us from the evil one'."*

As stated, there is so much in this prayer which can help shape our prayer life as disciples but I want to focus on the following six points.

Firstly, the prayer begins with the word *"Our"*. This is a clear reminder that praying is part of a community responsibility. While each disciple has a personal individual relationship with the Father through Jesus the Son, we are also part of a community. Our discipleship and our prayers can never flourish if we simply disengage from our part within the community, the Church, the body.

Secondly, the desire rooted in all prayer is to honour and revere God; this is the meaning of the word *"hallowed"*. The name of God is a key part of revelation: it is significant in terms of God making Himself known.[8]

Thirdly, there is a clear kingdom focus. The kingdom is to shape our agenda so also our prayers.[9]

Fourthly, while there is indeed a clear kingdom focus, there is also space for our own needs to be met. The reference to bread probably points to the necessities rather than the luxuries of life. However, the reference to bread may also direct our thinking to Jesus who is the bread of life (John 6:35).

Fifthly, an element of prayer is confession, and we have the reference to seeking forgiveness. Our own request for forgiveness seems closely linked to our willingness to forgive others.[10]

Sixthly and finally, the prayer recognises that as disciples we are in a 'spiritual battle', both in terms of our own sinful inclinations and in terms of the wider reality of evil. In this context both prayer and worship are vital and powerful spiritual weapons given to us as disciples. It is often through faithful prayer and Holy Spirit-inspired worship[11] that the power of God to overcome evil is released and experienced.

---

8. For a fuller reflection on the importance of God's name, see the book by R K Soulen - *The Divine Name(s) and the Holy Trinity* (volume 1) Westminster/John Knox Press, 2011.
9. We will explore having a kingdom focus when we look at Step Nine.
10. We will explore issues around forgiveness and forgiving when we look at Step Four.
11. We will explore worship further when we look at Step Six.

Points to consider

- What advice and encouragement would you give to a new disciple of Jesus in terms of growing in prayer?

- Reflect on the saying of St Francis de Sales (1567-1622): "Every Christian needs a half hour of prayer each day, except when he is busy, then he needs an hour."

STEP FOUR
Willing to Forgive

STEP FOUR – WILLING TO FORGIVE

Experiencing the gift of forgiveness is a key foundational point in our Christian experience. Every testimony of faith I have heard from a Christian has always had some focus on receiving and accepting forgiveness. This reality of forgiveness is based upon the atoning death of Jesus upon the cross.

In the previous section (Step Three), we noted how seeking forgiveness is a key element in the "sinner's prayer". Forgiveness and repentance are closely intertwined.

In the Gospel accounts of Jesus' life, we see many examples of His commitment to forgiveness. I will focus on three examples. Firstly, the account of Jesus being anointed by a sinful woman which is found in Luke 7:36-50. His forgiveness and affirmation of her transforms her, and it is also deeply challenging to the theological and cultural presuppositions of many of the Pharisees who were present. What we read here gives a wonderful glimpse into a beautiful encounter with Jesus. I think verse 44 is very insightful – namely the question Jesus asks of Simon: *"Do you see this woman?"* At one level clearly Simon did see her, but at a deeper level perhaps he never really did see her, because he had already judged her and dismissed her as a sinner, as an embarrassment and as an unwanted intruder -someone who should be ignored and made invisible. Simon remains blind to the real needs and worth of the woman, while Jesus truly sees, truly loves and fully forgives and restores. In Jesus, love and mercy triumph over judgement.

Secondly, the account of the woman caught in the very act of adultery.[1] This account in John 8, is deeply moving, and the compassionate love and wisdom of Jesus is demonstrated so astutely in His words of verse 7: *"...Let any one of you who is without sin be the first to throw a stone at her."* It is also worth noting that the religious authorities who brought the woman before Jesus did not bring the man. Maybe their concern for 'justice' was somewhat selective?

---

1. See John 8:2–11, (Some of the earliest Greek manuscripts do not have the text from John 7:53 to 8:11.)

Thirdly, the words of forgiveness Jesus spoke from the cross.[2] Here in the moment of the full horrors of crucifixion, in the very midst of physical agony and spiritual testing, Jesus ministers forgiveness. The Bible commentator Matthew Henry (1662-1714) writes powerfully about these words of Jesus: *"The sin they were now guilty of might justly have been made unpardonable. No, these are particularly prayed for. Now he made intercession for transgressors. Now the sayings of Christ upon the cross as well as his sufferings had a further intention than they seemed to have. This was explicatory of the intent and meaning of his death: "Father, forgive them, not only these, but all that shall repent, and believe the gospel." The great thing which Christ died to purchase and procure for us is the forgiveness of sin. His blood speaks this: Father forgive them. Though they were his persecutors and murderers, he prayed, Father forgive them."*[3]

Jesus demonstrates His readiness to forgive and this gives a context to His teaching and actions which also focused significantly on the importance and power of receiving and giving forgiveness. This teaching is found, for instance, in the LORD's prayer[4] where we glimpse the interconnectedness of receiving and giving forgiveness. Alongside this Jesus teaches a radical outworking of forgiveness in Matthew 5:38-39: *"You have heard that it was said, 'Eye for eye and tooth for tooth'. But I tell you, do not resist an evil person. If anyone slaps you on the right cheek, turn to them the other cheek also'."*

This emphasis on forgiveness, following on from the teaching and actions of Jesus, is then rooted in the practice of the early Church: for example, we read in Colossians 3:13[5]: *"Bear with each other and forgive one another if any of you has a grievance against someone. Forgive as the Lord forgave you."*

In the light of the example and teaching of Jesus, we as disciples must be active and willing to forgive those who have hurt us. We must also learn

---

2. See Luke 23:34.
3. Matthew Henry's, *Commentary on the whole Bible*, published by Marshall Pickering, 1960, p.296.
4. See Matthew 6:12.
5. See also Ephesians 4:32 and James 5:15.

to forgive ourselves. I think it is helpful to see prayers of forgiveness, not so much as occasional acts, but rather as an embedded attitude.

As disciples of Jesus, as forgiven people, we are called to forgive. Forgiving is an act of obedience and an essential outworking of discipleship. Sometimes forgiving comes easily, especially if the person who has hurt us recognises the hurt caused and shows sorrow and a desire to be reconciled with us. However, forgiving is often not easy. We may not feel like forgiving, as when we choose to forgive through 'gritted teeth'.

Forgiveness is an act of our will, which we need to constantly uphold. Sometimes, by God's grace these acts of forgiveness through 'gritted teeth' become easier over time. Rather than regularly remembering to and at times struggling to forgive, we begin gradually to forgive more 'freely' as forgiveness 'brings forth its fruits', and sometimes over time we begin to forget the hurt caused.

I think it is important to understand that forgiving is not the same as being reconciled. Forgiveness takes only one party or individual, while reconciliation involves at least two parties or individuals. Also, forgiveness is not saying that the hurt or injustice received does not matter. Sometimes it is right to be angry. However, as a disciple you are choosing not to act in revenge or hold tightly to the hurt and anger, but rather you are seeking to give the situation fully to the LORD.

In giving the hurt and anger to the LORD, I think it is helpful and, in some ways, essential to have in mind an 'eschatological perspective'. As a disciple of Jesus, I believe in the final judgement of God. This judgement will be full and perfect, and way beyond my calculations, personal vendettas, agendas or assumptions. This reality sets me free in the present from having, on the one hand to see (at whatever cost) full and perfect justice here and now, or on the other, falling into total despair as I see the injustices, brokenness and sufferings of the present age.

Practising forgiveness, (both as an individual disciple and as a Church community) alongside the pursuit of justice, is complex. True forgiveness is never based on indifference to injustice or ignoring abuse, but rather exercising genuine forgiveness means bringing the redemptive purposes of God into the context where forgiveness is needed. I hold strongly to the view that this does not in any way remove the priority from protecting the innocent, or from holding the guilty to account. The early Church wrestled with these questions. A good example of this is the way the command to love[6] and forgive[7] shapes the practice of the Church community and yet within the Church community, it is right to exercise appropriate judgement which can at times lead to acts of discipline and even exclusion.[8]

It is for the Church to discern when significant differences of opinion or specific attitudes or actions destroy the peace of the Church and undermine the proclamation of the Gospel. Yet the act of exclusion does not remove the responsibility to continue to love and pray for the one excluded. The community must be open to future possible reconciliation and reinstatement. We must learn to disagree well, and to do all we can to maintain unity and to live in fellowship yet, as the Bible and Church history reminds us, sometimes this cannot be faithfully achieved.

Each act of forgiveness is different and a range of diverse and powerful emotions such as fear, anger, hopelessness, sadness, and betrayal will be in play. Sometimes there is a wider context of control and coercion which needs to be named and confronted. Let me give one personal example: I once felt I was treated very poorly by my employer (and by some colleagues). I hope I have been able to forgive fully, but my desire to forgive did not mean I did not work hard to gain a fair severance arrangement. I also continue to hope that those involved in the decision against me will reflect and repent, both for their own growth and for the wellbeing of present and future employees.

When we are treated badly and perhaps our reputation is being trashed, other Christians often advise us to, 'let it go and move on' or 'fight for your rights', but rarely does either option seem like the best way to

---

6. See John 15:1-17, 1 Corinthians 13, 1 John 2:3-11 and 1 John 4:7-21
7. See Matthew 18:21-35 and Colossians 3:13.
8. See Matthew 18:15-18, 1 Corinthians 5 and 2 Corinthians 2:5-11.

proceed. I think there is often a middle way. To discern this 'middle way' we need the wisdom and empowering of the Holy Spirit. This wisdom and empowering will allow us to pursue godliness in challenging situations and to model a 'counter-cultural' goodness. This is far more nuanced than simply forgiving, forgetting or fighting for our rights. In all of this I think we must endeavour not to give up and, by God's grace, to be committed to speaking the 'truth in love' (especially to those in power) when opportunities arise. Never must anger or fear be allowed to shape our response. Never must acts of revenge take place, but we must seek to cultivate a deep sense of trust in the LORD. Such trust knows that truth, justice and mercy will triumph sometimes in this life- or if not, in the life to come.

Points to consider

- Talk with Christians you trust about their own experiences of receiving and giving forgiveness and how this connects with protecting the innocent and holding the guilty to account.
- Read the Book of Jonah. Reflect on chapter four and especially Jonah's anger at the LORD's compassion.

STEP FIVE
Willing to Go

STEP FIVE- WILLING TO GO

Discipleship involves action. The first action of discipleship is of essential importance, namely to come to Jesus. As stated, when we are considering the Biblical context of discipleship, the call by Jesus is always a call to Jesus, a call to follow and trust Him as Saviour and LORD. As disciples we are to be 'in Him', 'yielded to Him' and 'renewed through Him'. The apostle Paul summed this up in the key phrase 'united with Christ', and Jesus Himself taught this truth by depicting our relationship with Him in terms of a vine and branches (John 15).

Each disciple needs to be 'rooted in Jesus', and a disciple is called 'to be' before he or she is called 'to go' or called 'to do'. Our identity and status are always found in Christ rather than in our actions, connections or achievements. However, each disciple needs to hear the call of Jesus 'to go.' This willingness to respond to this call, to be obedient, to be ready to leave the familiar and the safe, is a core component of discipleship.

We see this core component being put in place throughout the teaching ministry of Jesus. For example, in Matthew 10:1-42, Jesus prepares the 'Twelve' to go out on a mission by giving them authority and clear instructions. The instructions here give specific details about what to bring, what to say and what to do. There is also a direct instruction for the twelve disciples to focus solely upon reaching out to the lost sheep of Israel (Matthew 10:6). Later in Matthew 28:16-20,[1] this 'mission call' is deepened and enlarged with these words (often referred to as the great commission): *"Then Jesus came to them and said, 'All authority in heaven and on earth has been given to me. Therefore go and make disciples of all nations, baptising them in the name of the Father and of the Son and of the Holy Spirit, and teaching them to obey everything I have commanded you. And surely I am with you always, to the very end of the age."*

In Matthew 28:16-20, I understand that there are four key connected actions which are foundational to faithful mission activity. Firstly,

---

[1]. Chapter 28 is the concluding chapter of Matthew's Gospel and most commentators understand that this 'great commission' is the chosen climax of Matthew's account of the person and work of Jesus.

'going'; secondly, 'making' (make disciples); thirdly, 'marking' (baptising them); and fourthly, 'maturing' (teaching them). This commission is made possible and sustained by the wonderful promise that the presence of Jesus will always be with His disciples.

The outworking of this great commission and the assurance of the LORD's presence is demonstrated throughout the Book of Acts. The Book of Acts is in some ways 'the bridge' between the Gospel accounts and the development of the 'early Church'. In Acts 1:8 we read: *"... you will receive power when the Holy Spirit[2] comes on you; and you will be my witnesses in Jerusalem, and in all Judea, and Samaria, and to the ends of the earth."*

The structure of the Book of Acts is based upon this 'missional going,' beginning in Jerusalem and going out in stages to the very edges of the known world. Luke, the author of the Book of Acts, gives a challenging and inspiring account of the faith and life of the early Church. It is a book about a community which becomes a movement.

This movement begins with 120 Jewish believers in Jesus waiting fearfully in Jerusalem, yet also waiting faithfully for the promised coming of the Holy Spirit, and it concludes with Paul preaching and teaching the good news of Jesus freely (yet under house arrest) in Rome— Rome, then being the very epicentre of the most powerful empire, the world has ever known.

Acts is about a missionary journey (mainly in a western direction from Jerusalem to Rome). This journey has distinct parts. These parts reflect the great commission given by Jesus in Matthew 28. For example, Acts 8 is focused on how the Gospel takes root in Samaria. Samaria is an important 'stepping stone' or 'bridge community' halfway between the Jewish context of Jerusalem and the wider mainly pagan, predominantly Gentile Roman world. This halfway context helpfully shows that God does not 'parachute' us as disciples into 'impossible' situations but leads us step by step, beginning where we are (Jerusalem) and taking us forward, enabling us to grow and learn in partly familiar contexts

---

2. The Holy Spirit confirms the presence and power of the risen Jesus with His people.

(Samaria) before enlarging our expectations and assumptions and opening up pioneering new worlds (to the ends of the earth).

This sense of movement, of being obedient to discern and obey the call of God, connects us as contemporary disciples with the faithful 'pilgrim people' of the Jewish faith narrative. It connects us with people such as Abraham, who heard and obeyed the call to go, as Genesis 12:1 reads: *"The Lord had said to Abram,*[3] *'Go from your country, your people and your father's household to the land I will show you',"* and also with people such as Moses (Exodus chapters 2 and 3), Joshua (Joshua chapter 1) and the prophet Jeremiah (Jeremiah chapter 1). We can learn so much from these faithful people.

My own personal reflection on this sense of movement, of a person's willingness to 'go', is that I have found that, when I as a disciple have a sense of movement and am committed to some key activity, it is far easier for me to discern God's will and to recognise the promptings of the Holy Spirit, than the times when I have been largely static, passive, or set in my ways. There is a saying which I have found to be especially challenging and true: *"It is far easier to steer a moving car than a parked one."*

One final reflection on the call to go: sometimes the faithful response is to stay. It can sometimes be easier to leave difficult or challenging situations and seek to move on to the 'next new thing'[4] while the LORD is calling us to stand firm and to honour the commitments we have made and to be firmly rooted. Perhaps the account in Luke 8 gives us a helpful glimpse of this truth. In Luke 8:38-39, the man who had been healed from demon possession begs to go with Jesus, but Jesus tells him to return home and to stay as a witness of what Jesus has done for him. As always there is a challenging balance between going (in obedience) and staying (in obedience). To be faithful needs great discernment; but the willingness to go remains a key mark of discipleship.

---

3. Abram is renamed Abraham following the events (the covenant of circumcision) of Genesis 17. See Genesis 17:5.

4. Do not confuse the allure of novelty with the genuine move of the Holy Spirit.

Points to consider

- Can you think of examples when you have sensed the LORD's calling to go into a new situation in order to serve Him and grow as a disciple?

- In recognising and responding to God's call we all face the need to decide carefully and act faithfully. For me this often seems to involve discerning the balance between the following:

    Self-confidence and arrogance

    Enthusiasm and fanaticism

    Ambition and contentment

    Idealism and naivety

    Helpfulness and interference

    Enjoyment and excess

    Compassion and sentimentality.

- Pray that the LORD will help you to discern the way forward and to navigate carefully your next steps.

STEP SIX
Focusing on Worship

STEP SIX- FOCUSING ON WORSHIP

Worship is the faithful response to God's presence. It is rooted in a sense of wonder. Abraham Heschel, writes: *"The surest way to suppress our ability to understand the meaning of God and the importance of worship is to take things for granted. Indifference to the sublime wonder of living is the root of sin."*[1]

It is hard to capture the fullness of worship, I have however found this definition by William Temple (1881-1944) helpful and inspiring: *"To worship is to quicken the conscience by the holiness of God. To feed the mind with the truth of God. To purge the imagination by the beauty of God. To devote the will to the purpose of God."*

Throughout the Bible there are a number of key Hebrew words which are usually translated into English as worship, praise or service. The Hebrew word '*Shachah*' is the most frequent and literally means to bow, kneel or prostrate oneself in homage. This word is used firstly in Genesis 22:5.

In the New Testament there are also a number of key Greek words which are usually translated into English as 'worship'. The Greek verb '*Proskuneo*' is the most frequent (60 uses) and as with the Hebrew word '*Shachah*' points to paying homage by kneeling or prostration. These actions flow from inner feelings or thoughts of reverence and awe. Literally the word means to draw near in order to kiss.

The verb '*Latreuo*' (22 uses) points to an act of religious service, paying homage and the offering of gifts. The verb '*Sebomai*'(10 uses) has a primary meaning of reverence. To revere with a sense of devotion and humility.

This initial brief word study will hopefully have given us some glimpses into the depth and intimacy of worship. However, as we humble ourselves and focus on God's presence and promises, and also on God's greatness and goodness, the experience of worship goes beyond words and theological concepts. We enter into the life of the Spirit. This is why

---

1. Abraham Heschel, *God in Search of Man*, p.43

Jesus taught[2] that true worship is always empowered by and embedded in the Holy Spirit and in truth.

God wants disciples to live in His presence – this is true worship. The opposite of true worship is idolatry. Clearly as disciples we aspire in all aspects of our living to offer worship. However, in most contexts, we see the offering of worship as focused primarily, but never exclusively, on the set times when we gather with other Christians,[3] with a focus on praising God for His saving acts.

Such gatherings can be a mixture of the structured, liturgical and the formal alongside the spontaneous. There is no set formula, but Christian worship is built upon the key building blocks of praise, thanksgiving and adoration. Often these 'building blocks' act as a catalyst for times of fellowship enriched by singing, praying, reading and proclaiming Scripture, making offerings, celebrating Holy communion,[4] sharing testimonies, using spiritual gifts, times of confession, silent contemplation, acts of reconciliation and welcoming new disciples, especially through the sacrament of baptism.

It is a core element of discipleship to be committed to a community of Christians and to be faithful in sharing in regular public times of worship. It is sometimes not easy for a new disciple to know which Church community to belong to. As a general rule, it is wise to commit to a Church where Jesus and the work of the Holy Spirit are central to the teaching and worship. Also, it is good to be part of a community in which you are warmly welcomed and you can both receive and begin to learn to serve. It is also often important that the Church is rooted in your local community.

Worship and service are signs of commitment, and the more you commit the stronger your relationships within your Church will grow. As stated earlier, there is no set formula for acts of public worship, and there is much diversity – rooted in both local traditions and Holy Spirit inspired

---

2. See John 4:24.
3. See Matthew 18:20, 1 Corinthians 14:26 and Colossians 3:15–17.
4. Also known in a range of Christian traditions as the Lord's Supper, Passover meal, Mass, and the Eucharist.

initiatives. However, the core purpose must be honoured: namely, worship is the joyful acknowledgement of the saving acts of God and is the desire to make the reality of these acts known in the lives of all who participate.

Throughout Christian history, worship has preceded and shaped theological formulation. For example, the very earliest Christians freely worshipped Jesus as LORD well before any overarching doctrinal statements about His person and nature had been established. Thus, it can be seen that early confessions of doctrine flowed from Holy Spirit led worship. A good example of this would be the hymn of praise to Christ[5] in Philippians 2:5-11, which Paul is almost certainly quoting from a well-known source, because this 'hymn' was so widely known within the emerging Christian communities. So, we see that the truth is that worship is the reason for theology,[6] and all true theological developments end in praise.

In reflecting on the primacy of worship, I have found the writing of Christopher Watkin very insightful. Watkin claims that: *"A Christian engagement with truth, goodness or beauty that does not end in praise is missing something, like visiting the Venice opera and spending the entire performance studying the programme."* [7]

Points to consider

- What has helped or hindered you in your worship?

- Read and reflect upon descriptions of worship in Revelation 4:1-11, 7:9-17 and 19:1-10.

- David Hart in his book The Beauty of the Infinite, writes: "The most fully adequate discourse of truth is worship." Do you agree with this and, if so, why?

---

5. This is generally referred to as the *'Carmen Christi'*.
6. My own working definition of theology is that theology is faith and worship seeking understanding.
7. Christopher Watkin, *Biblical Critical Theory*, p.602.

STEP SEVEN
Committing to Study

STEP SEVEN - COMMITTING TO STUDY

A commitment to life-long study is a key part of life-long discipleship. To study in order to gain knowledge is very important, yet at the pinnacle of Christian study is not the desire to gain knowledge simply to comprehend, or in order to use, but to be able to fully revere God and His creation.

There are many Biblical texts which encourage this commitment to study, to memorize and to reflect.[1] Let's begin by seeing two examples. Firstly, Joshua 1:8 reads: *"Keep this Book of the Law always on your lips; meditate on it day and night, so that you may be careful to do everything written in it..."*. Secondly, Proverbs 3:1 reads: *"My son, do not forget my teaching, but keep my commands in your heart."*

2 Timothy 2:15 is also a key text in this regard as well, the verse reads: *"Do your best to present yourself to God as one approved, a worker who does not need to be ashamed and who correctly handles the word of truth."* This verse refers to knowing God's word and being able to use God's word in order to call out false philosophies and teachings. Yet it applies to our wider education as well. As disciples we should commit to whatever area of study or work, we are involved in, in order to serve others and to be the best we can be.

The commitment to study is rooted in Biblical tradition, yet we should be aware of falsely honouring learning as an end in itself and in taking a false pride in our own 'cleverness'. St Anselm observed: *"God often works more by the illiterate seeking the things of God than the learned seeking the things that are their own."* St Augustine of Hippo, in his confessions said something very similar, namely: *"See how the unlearned start up and take heaven by storm, whilst we with all our learning grovel upon the earth."*

As disciples, potential areas of study are endless and there are infinite insights to be gained and knowledge to be examined, applied and valued. I am encouraged and deeply thankful to know that there are faithful Christians excelling in every area of science, medicine, psychology, economics, engineering, computing, politics, linguistics, jurisprudence,

---

[1]. See Proverbs 1:7 and 18:15, Matthew 11:29, John 14:15–17, and Romans 15:4.

philosophy, ethics, architecture, business, history, and all the creative arts. However, in this brief section on committing to study, I will focus on one foundational area of Christian study, namely, studying the Bible.

As a disciple of Jesus, I recognise and seek to uphold that the Bible is the supreme authority for what I believe and how I try and live. 2 Timothy 3:16 proclaims that *"All Scripture is God-breathed and is useful for teaching, rebuking, correcting, and training in righteousness."* This authority flows from the sovereignty of God. God is sovereign not just in His engagement with creation and people, but also in His revelation of Himself to people. The Bible not only informs, but has the power to reform and to transform. The Bible is, I believe, a component part in the redeeming work of God, as the Bible accurately makes known God's ways and actions. In addition, the Bible teaches how people should respond to God's actions. Therefore, how we as disciples value, study, read, preach and apply the message of the Biblical text is of foundational importance.

As a disciple I have come to value the following six steps which have greatly helped me to study the Bible over many years - in ways which I have found to be creative, sustainable, informative and inspiring.

Firstly, I need to understand that God wants to make His revelation through the Bible clear to me. The truths of the Bible are consistent and are open to all who sincerely seek understanding and direction. This truth is based not primarily on my efforts or ability but upon the work of the Holy Spirit. The Holy Spirit, who is central to the process of revelation (2 Timothy 3:16 and 2 Peter 1:20-21), will help illuminate and embed the message of the text to every sincere reader and every earnest seeker of truth.

Secondly, I need to set aside time and find a suitable place to carefully study the text. I also need a translation of the text which helps me firstly to understand, and then apply, what I am reading.

Thirdly, I need to persevere in my study. This is a life-long task. Over the years I have found it useful to begin any study by trying to assess the grammatical, historical and textual context of the text or texts alongside questions about authorship, place and date of writing.

In general, a text should be interpreted by its most straightforward meaning. Words should be interpreted consistently in the same context. A word can have different meanings, but only one correct meaning in each case in terms of the author's intent. It is also helpful, in exploring meaning, to compare one passage with other Biblical texts on related themes. For example, if I am studying 1 John 4:7-12 and thinking about how we should love others, it would be helpful to also read John 15:12-13, 1 Peter 4:8-9 and 1 Corinthians 13. I do this because I understand one part of the Bible can help interpret, refine and affirm another part of the Bible.[2]

Fourthly, I need to invest time not simply in studying on my own, but to do so with other disciples. Group study can be vital in gaining new insights and in beginning to see how the truths of the Bible are shaping other people (who are often very different from myself) and helping them flourish as disciples. It is also good in times of study to learn from those who have particular gifts and experience in teaching and supporting others. We can all learn much from such gifted and authorised leaders, scholars, teachers, preachers and pastors.

Fifthly, study must lead to action. I need to try to apply insights to my own decision-making and to my lifestyle. Sometimes the application of a text is very straightforward. It may not be easy, but it is clear. At other times an obvious application is not apparent. In seeking to 'live out the text' we are following the teaching in James 1:22 which reads: *"Do not merely listen to the word, and so deceive yourselves. Do what it says."*

Finally, I need to make time in order to reflect upon what I am learning and how I (and others) have understood and applied a text. Maybe my reflection confirms my understanding and application, but equally it is possible that I may have misunderstood or misused the text in some way. I need to persevere and to be humble and open. I need to recognise I never stop learning, and I always need the gentle leading of the Holy Spirit in order to be faithful to the revelation of the Bible, and to make astute choices in living faithfully as a disciple.

---

2. This method is known as the interpretive principle of correlation.

Points to consider

- I often pray the following before I begin to study the Bible: "LORD, help me to understand your word today. Set me free from any false worldviews or any false insights. Please renew my mind, and enlarge my heart so I can receive your truth and direction."

- What advice would you give to a new disciple who is beginning to study the Bible for the first time?

- Try to memorize some Bible verses which you have been encouraged by.

STEP EIGHT
Recognising your Gifting

STEP EIGHT - RECOGNISING YOUR GIFTINGS

The Holy Spirit is at work in every disciple. Gifts of ministry and service are given to every disciple: such giving is always the initiative of the Holy Spirit and an outworking of the grace of God. In order to grow as a disciple and to function faithfully in the body of Christ it is important to cultivate an attitude of confidence and expectation in the equipping which flows from the Holy Spirit.

Each disciple, alongside some of the gifts given by the Holy Spirit, will have their own natural gifts, abilities, and skills acquired and developed over time. These natural gifts and skills are also from God. All of this is then mixed within our unique personalities and shaped by relationships, circumstances and contexts. In the world where God is all powerful and all present it is hard to distinguish between supernatural gifts (gifts of the Holy Spirit) and other gifts and skills. In almost every ministry setting faithful service is a mixture of all of these elements. However, in this brief section I focus on what are mostly understood within a Christian context as spiritual (supernatural) gifts.

In terms of spiritual gifts, focus is usually placed on the nine gifts listed in 1 Corinthians 12:8-10. These are wisdom, knowledge, faith, healing, miraculous power, prophecy, discernment, speaking in tongues and the interpretation of tongues. However, other lists of gifts are also given. For example, in Romans 12 there is a focus on prophecy, acts of service, teaching, giving encouragement, giving generously, leadership and showing mercy. In Ephesians 4 the focus is on the ministry position (apostle, prophet, evangelist and pastor/teacher) someone holds rather than on a specific activity or gifting. In addition, there is mention of voluntary celibacy (1 Corinthians 7:7) poverty and martyrdom (1 Corinthians 13:3). In exercising all of these gifts the indispensable context is always love (1 Corinthians 13). There is clearly a wide range of spiritual gifts being used within the early Church community and these are mentioned in the New Testament. It is possible that the New Testament does not list every gift the Holy Spirt gives and there may have been other gifts and other recognised ministries within the life of the early Church.

It is good to recognise the gift, or gifts, we have and to seek to use them wisely. Paul tells Timothy: *"Do not neglect your gift, which was given you through prophecy when the body of elders laid their hands on you"* (1 Timothy 4:14). The correct remedy for neglect is to use, to stir up again and to celebrate. The Message translation of this verse also gives a helpful insight: *"...And that special gift of ministry you were given when the leaders of the church laid hands on you and prayed – keep that dusted off and in use."*

In addition to not neglecting what we have been given, it is also good to seek additional gifts, to be open to whatever the LORD seeks to give us in order to help us to love Him more deeply and serve Him more effectively. However, in seeking spiritual gifting, we need to be focused not on the gift but always on the Giver, for the heart of the Holy Spirit's work is to reveal the fullness of God to us. The one true God, Father, Son and Holy Spirit.[1]

In reflecting on these gifts, we need to understand that they are gifts of grace. They are not earned by our service, or given based on maturity. They are not to be viewed as medals to be paraded or badges of honour to be owned, but rather as tools of service -tools to be used and shared. The purpose of God in giving gifts to you is that He might do something through you and by so doing bring blessings to others.

Sometimes, very sadly gifts may be misused and, rather than been used effectively in ministry motivated by love, they are used to boost someone's pride or to manipulate or control someone else. This is shameful. Often the response to such misuse is for Church communities to shy away from a focus on using and affirming spiritual gifts. While this is an understandable reaction, the Biblical response to this misuse is never non-use, but always to seek right use. Right use involves sensitivity, love and discernment. It means working closely with other

---

1. For a helpful introduction into the understanding of God, Father Son and Holy Spirit, with a focus on the divinity of Jesus, see my book, *Walking an Ancient Path*. Details in bibliography.

Christians and having appropriate levels of accountability. As gifts are used and ministries grow, it is important that the 'fruit of the Spirit' (Galatians 5:22) is also cultivated in our lives and in our Church communities. The gifts and fruit of the Spirit are closely linked, and the outpouring of the Holy Spirit is linked to the events of Pentecost (Acts 2). This outpouring is a sign of the kingdom and the first steps of recovery of what was lost in the Fall (Genesis 3).

While the focus is clearly upon the work of the Holy Spirit, it is helpful to understand that Paul's teaching in 1 Corinthians 12 links each person of the Trinity (Father, Son and Holy Spirit) to the outworking of spiritual gifts. In 1 Corinthians 12:4 Paul writes: *"There are different kinds of gifts, but the same Spirit distributes them. There are different kinds of service, but the same Lord. There are different kinds of working, but in all of them and in everyone it is the same God at work."* When a disciple uses the gifts, he or she has freely received, the fullness of God (Father, Son and Holy Spirit) is working in that disciple for the blessing and well-being of others.

Points to consider

- Thank God for the gifts, abilities and skills you have. Ask God to show you how these can be used wisely and joyfully in His service.

- Find some time and a quiet space to read John 14:15 to John 15:17. Pray that the LORD will help you to draw close to Him.

STEP NINE
Seeking the Kingdom

STEP NINE- SEEKING THE KINGDOM

In the early part of this book, I outlined the Biblical context of discipleship and made the case that discipleship is linked directly to the kingdom of God. This I believe is explicit in the teaching of Jesus, where the kingdom of God is the message and discipleship is the method. With this understanding it is clear that in regard to the decisions we make and 'lifestyles' we seek to model, it is of primary importance that we are 'in step' with kingdom values and are seeking kingdom goals. Lifestyle involves more than just what we do: it includes our identity, our relationships, ambitions, thoughts, attitudes, words and habits.

In focusing on the kingdom of God we are, as disciples, engaging with the concept which unifies all of the Bible. It is the central theme which gives coherence to our theology and to the outworking of our faith.

Daniel Holland writes: *"The Kingdom of God is a place where you have freedom and encouragement to grow closer to Jesus, and to others who love Him. You will find you are now meeting with people you would never otherwise have had anything to do with. The beauty of the Kingdom is that as we get closer to Jesus, we draw nearer to other Christians who love Jesus. We need to be Jesus-focused; this is our best hope for good relationships. Socio-economic background, political views and culture recede. All the usual divisions and prejudices start to fall away. This is wonderful evidence of God's work."*[1]

Kingdom living is a recognition that our lives are in God's hands. James 4:13-17 makes clear that it is sheer foolishness mixed with arrogance to boast about and pursue our own agendas. A similar point is made in the parable of the rich fool as told in Luke 12:13-21.

In seeking 'first the kingdom' we are putting into practice the clear instruction of Jesus. Matthew 6:33 reads: "*...seek first*[2] *his kingdom and his righteousness...*". The context here is one of trust. We can trust Jesus to meet our daily needs

---

1. Daniel Holland, *A practical handbook- Growing as a new Christian*, published by Christian Publications International, 2022, p.25.

2. The Greek grammar of this verse is written in the present continuous tense, so it means seek first and keep on seeking first. The same grammatical rule is in place in Romans 1:16 in regards to "*...first to the Jew*".

as we try and prioritise the kingdom. At the heart of the kingdom is loving like Jesus loved. Throughout His ministry He prioritised the way of love over self-interest. He followed His Father's will, fully and perfectly. The prime example of all of this is His willingness to go to the cross.

In seeking the kingdom as disciples, we are not seeking to live by our own agendas or vanities, but we are seeking to put Jesus and the things which have lasting spiritual value first in our lives. The key values of the kingdom are intertwined with the gifts and fruit of the Holy Spirit.[3]

Each disciple endeavouring to seek and live out the kingdom will have different insights and individual responsibilities and callings. Nevertheless, there will always be strong evidence of the following: honouring Jesus, proclaiming the truth, working in partnership with others, pursuing peace with justice, exercising faith, trust, honesty, humility, generosity, and a deep transforming love for others. This will then be enriched by having concern for the vulnerable and the 'outsider' along with compassion and identification with those who suffer. There will also be joy in seeing the achievements of others, alongside many times of 'infectious' celebration. Celebration based upon the grace and goodness of God. As we explore the gift of grace, we learn that the bedrock of all hope is belief in the grace of God.

There are clearly so many core kingdom values and actions to explore, but I will focus here on just one, humility. In terms of humility, we are reminded that a disciple is never seeking personal greatness, but is seeking the LORD. We see the outworking of humility in the ministry of Jesus. This humility is powerfully declared in Philippians 2:5-11 which reads: "*In your relationship with one another, have the same mindset as Christ Jesus: who, being in the very nature God, did not consider equality with God something to be used to his own advantage; rather, he made himself nothing by taking the very nature of a servant, being made in human likeness. And being found in appearance as a man, he humbled himself by becoming obedient to death – even death on a cross! Therefore God exalted him to the highest place and gave him the name that is above every name, that at the name of Jesus every knee should bow, in heaven and on earth and under the earth, and every*

---

3. See Step Eight.

tongue acknowledge that Jesus Christ is Lord, to the glory of God the Father."

We also see this humility in Moses. Moses is described in Numbers 12:3 as: *"...a very humble man, more humble than anyone else on the face of the earth."* Why was Moses so humble? I understand that this was because he saw the greatness and glory of God.

In terms of living out kingdom values a disciple will see many signs of God's power and love in action. The kingdom is here in the present. Yet also many aspects of the kingdom are still waiting to be established. The kingdom is here, but not yet: there is a kingdom reality, but this reality is not fully established.

As disciples we navigate a world which is full of God's goodness, beauty, joy and blessing yet also a world of decay, injustice, sin, suffering and death. There is this 'now but not yet' tension of the kingdom which every disciple both wrestles with and acknowledges. This acknowledgement is rooted both in terms of one's own personal issues and struggles, and in the wider realities of living in the world.

There is a celebration of God's power and love here and now, but also a deep longing for what will be when the LORD returns and the old order of things will pass away and all will be made new![4] Christopher Watkin makes this point compellingly and writes: *"By the grace of God I am what I am, and what I shall be has not yet been made known (1 Cor 15:10; 1 John 3:2). In a late modern culture that rhymes complete self-expression with authenticity and places a heavy burden on selves to become transparent and fully actualized, I know that as a Christian I need not to be crushed by the obligation of having fully to express, or even fully to understand myself here and now. If I remain torn between different identities, if I remain frustrated by who I am until the moment of my death, I know just like the carnivorous lion who will lie down with the lamb and yet be more lion than ever, there awaits for me a subversive fulfilment of the tangled knot of my desires, assumptions, blind spots and predispositions that will surprise, delight, and fulfil me in ways I never dreamed possible."*[5]

---

4. See Revelation 21:1-5.
5. Christopher Watkin, *Biblical Critical Theory*, published by Zondervan, 2022, p.578.

What Watkins reminds us is that, as disciples of the risen and returning LORD, the end gives retrospective meaning to the whole. So, as we seek the kingdom and keep on seeking the kingdom in terms of our values, choices, goals and actions, there will be a growing sense of fulfilment and purpose in this life, and a renewed hope as we begin to glimpse the 'life everlasting'.

Points to consider

- In seeking 'first the kingdom' what changes do you think you may need to make in the short and longer term?

- Where do you see signs of the kingdom in your community?

- The hymn God of grace and God of glory[6] contains this verse: "Heal the children's warring madness; bend our pride to thy control: shame our wanton, selfish gladness, rich in things and poor in soul. Grant us wisdom, grant us courage, lest we miss thy kingdom's goal." Spend some time reflecting and trying to memorize this verse.

---

6. Composed by H E Fosdick (1878–1969).

STEP TEN
Keeping on Going

STEP TEN - KEEPING ON GOING

Discipleship is a life-long commitment. Yet sometimes every disciple experiences significant times of disappointment, hurt, bereavement, suffering, confusion or failure which can undermine commitment and even make us want to give up. At times such as this, we need to seek the LORD anew and stand firm. There is a very special saying which I have been greatly encouraged by during a number of testing times: the saying is this: *"If I stand, LORD, let me stand on the promise that you will pull me through – and if I can't, let me fall on the grace that first brought me to you."*

It is important to remember that our security as Christians is never found from holding on in our own strength, but from knowing that it is the LORD who holds us.

The importance of perseverance, of keeping on going, is taught throughout the Bible. A good starting place is the parable of the persistent widow (Luke 18:1-8). Here Jesus encourages His disciples to persevere in prayer. If an unfaithful judge, who shows little commitment to what is right or wrong, is compelled by badgering to act fairly towards a helpless widow, how much more will God hear the cries of His people and act graciously. Also in this parable, the final verse (v.8) switches the context to the return (second coming) of the LORD. The time leading up to His return is understood in the Bible as a time of significant spiritual apathy, decline and persecution (Matthew 24:1-35). Therefore, having a faith and lifestyle which perseveres in such a testing context is of vital importance.

Robert Gordon[1] writes helpfully about the need for perseverance in the context of prayer. He reflects on the persistence of the friend who arrives at midnight (Luke 11:5-8) and writes: *"Often it is our sense of timing that needs re-adjustment. What we thought was of the utmost priority is seen in the light of God's timing to be less urgent. Sometimes I think it takes time to show us the exact measure of the problem involved. We start praying at one level but as we persist, we are shown in our spirit that there is much more to the question than we had first thought. One thing is clear, God wants us to*

---

1. Robert (Bob) Gordon, 1942-1997, was a pioneering Bible teacher and taught widely on discipleship and the gifts of the Holy Spirit.

persevere so that he can release what he wills into our lives. *Some words of John Wesley, that sound quaint to our ears nowadays, makes the same point: 'Storm the throne of grace and persevere therein, and mercy will come down'."*²

We also see such perseverance and determination in the person of Jesus, especially as He approaches the reality of the cross. We see this in Luke 9:51, where Jesus resolutely and with unwavering determination sets out to Jerusalem and then, in Luke 22:39-46, we see how Jesus perseveres through a time of great anguish and suffering in order to 'keep in step' with the will of His father.

In the Letter of James³ we are given the example of Job. James 5:11 reads: *"As you know, we count as blessed those who have persevered. You have heard of Job's perseverance and have seen what the Lord finally brought about. The Lord is full of compassion and mercy."*

Traditionally we link Job with patience, but it is his perseverance which is celebrated both here, by James, and in the Book of Job itself.⁴

We can also find many wonderful and challenging examples of perseverance throughout the history of the Church. In the introduction to this book I mentioned how Dietrich Bonhoeffer inspired and challenged me. However, there are many other Christians, who have also inspired and challenged me. Some I have known personally and there are others I have known through reading or hearing about their lives. Let me share, just one example with you; this is the Rev William Henry Hechler (1845-1931).

William was born in Benares, India, and had a German-English heritage. After his mother's death (he was aged only five when this occurred), he was educated in boarding schools in London and in Switzerland. His father (Dietrich Hechler) became an Anglican Minister and missionary and clearly influenced young William in a number of important ways. William was ordained as an Anglican Minister in 1870

---

2. Robert Gordon, *How much More shall your Father give the Holy Spirit to them that ask him*, published by Marshalls, 1983, p.83.
3. James is a brother of Jesus. This letter is probably the earliest New Testament writing around 45 AD.
4. See Job 1:20-22, 2:7-10 and 13:15. Job provides a prime example of perseverance.

and gained a reputation as a leading Biblical scholar and renowned linguist - he spoke at least ten languages. He had a range of ministry roles as a mission worker in Nigeria, tutor to the children of Grand Duke Frederick of Baden and as chaplain to the British Embassy in Vienna. He married and had four children.

Through his Biblical studies he developed a deep understanding of God's faithful love for Jewish people and of the Biblical prophetic promises to restore the Jewish people to Palestine.[5] He travelled widely and was shocked and heart-broken by the violent pogroms he saw initiated mainly by the Russian state against the Jewish people. He became a strong advocate against all forms of antisemitism and met with, and encouraged many, of the early Zionist pioneers, including Leon Pinsker and most significantly Theodor Herzl. He also met with many key European leaders and provided Herzl with many opportunities to promote the emerging Zionist vision. William was an activist and a Christian mystic. Some may argue William was somewhat eccentric, yet he had a profound insight into the geo-political realities of his time and how these related to the teaching, interpretation and application of the Bible.

Despite his determined efforts and life-long perseverance William saw none of his hopes fulfilled. The key partnership with Herzl ended when Herzl died suddenly aged just 44. Also, the bond between Germany and Britain which William treasured was torn apart in the horrors of the First World War. He warned tirelessly against the folly of this war and worked to avoid it. Following this he warned against the rise of Nazism and he foresaw the horrors of the Holocaust. His warnings and insights were ignored and he was sidelined.

It was as if the 'tide of history' was flowing against all of William's deepest hopes, dreams and understandings. However, he remained resolute and faithful. He went on writing and teaching, and developed an important friendship with the great philosopher Martin Buber. He kept on keeping on!

---

5. William Hechler wrote in 1884 the influential book, *The Restoration of the Jews to Palestine*.

William Henry Hechler died alone, in 1931, and was buried in an unmarked grave. His life was largely forgotten. Yet this was not the end. Seventeen years later and following the horrors of the Holocaust, the State of Israel was established (May 1948) and in 2010 his unmarked grave was 'rediscovered' and a graveside memorial erected at a special service in January 2011. I was privileged to be at this service, and during this event I met many people, including a good number of Jewish Believers in Jesus, for whom William Hechler is a prime example of visionary Christian discipleship and a model of faithful perseverance.

In reflecting on our own lives and the life of William Hechler, it is clearly hard to know what results, if any, we as disciples will see through our own faithful perseverance, or how any of our acts of discipleship or visionary hopes will find their fulfilment. However, as we draw this study with its Ten Steps to its conclusion, let us be encouraged and let me give the final word to Dietrich Bonhoeffer, who poses this foundational question: "And *if we answer the call to discipleship, where will it lead us? What decisions and partings will it demand? To answer this question, we shall have to go to him, for only he knows the answer. Only Jesus Christ, who bids us to follow him, knows the journey's end. But we do know that it will be a road of boundless mercy. Discipleship means joy.*"[6]

Points to consider

- Can you give an example of where your road of discipleship has been a road of boundless mercy?

- I gave the example of William Hechler as a Christian from history who has inspired me. Who would you select as your example, and why?

- What have you found most encouraging and challenging in this book on discipleship?

---

6. Dietrich Bonhoeffer, *The Cost of Discipleship*, SCM Press, 2019, p.xxxiv.

BIBLIOGRAPHY

Listed below are all the books I have referenced; plus, some other books I have found useful for background study and/or for further reflection.

Biale David, *Hasidism–A New History*, Princeton University Press, 2018.

Bonhoeffer Dietrich, *The Cost of Discipleship*, first published in German (1937), SCM Press, 2019.

Bosanquet Mary, *Bonhoeffer-True Patriot*, Mowbrays, 1968.

Brunner Emil, *The Christian Doctrine of God* (Dogmatics Volume 1), Westminster Press, 1950.

Buchanan Stuart, *Called by God?* SPCK, 2008.

Butler-Gallie Fergus, *Priests De La Resistance!* Oneworld Publications, 2019.

Collier Winn, *A Burning in my Bones – Authorized Biography of Eugene H. Peterson*, Authentic Media, 2020.

Cotterell Tracey and Hudson Neil, *Leading a Whole-Life Disciplemaking Church*, Grove Books, 2012.

Foster Richard, *Prayer*, Hodder and Stoughton, 1992.

Gordon Robert, *'How much more shall your Father give the Holy Spirit to them that ask him'*, Marshalls, 1983.

Hart David, *The Beauty of the Infinite*, Eerdmans, 2004.

Henry Matthew, *Commentary on the Whole Bible*, Marshall Pickering, 1960.

Heschel Abraham, *God in Search of Man*, Farrar, Straus and Giroux, 1953.

Holland Daniel, *A practical handbook- Growing as a new Christian*, Christian Publications International, 2022.

Jacob Alex, *Walking an Ancient Path*, Glory to Glory Publications, 2016.
    100 Days with Luke, Christian Publications International, 2018.
    100 Days with Acts, Christian Publications International, 2019.
    60 Days with Romans, Christian Publications Internation, 2020.

Jeremias Joachim, *The Prayers of Jesus*, SCM Press, 2012.

John J and Walley Chris, *Jesus Christ – The Truth*, Philo Trust, 2019.

Loscalzo Craig, *Apologetic Preaching*, Inter-Varsity Press, 2000.

Lowenthal Marvin, *The Dairies of Theodor Herzl*, Dial Press, 1956.

Peterson Eugene, *Under the Unpredictable Plant*, Eerdmans Publishing, 1992.

Roberts Andrew, Humphries Deborah, Johnson Neil and Milton Tom (Editors) *Holy Habits* (a teaching series of ten), The Bible Reading Fellowship, 2018.

Singlehurst Laurence, *Sowing Reaping, Keeping*, Inter-Varsity Press, 1995.

Soulen R K, *The Divine Name(s) and the Holy Trinity* (Volume 1), Westminster/John Knox Press, 2011.

Vlach Michael, *He Will Reign Forever*, Lampion House, 2017.

Warren Norman, *Journey into Life*, CPAS/Kingsway, 1990.

Watkin Christopher, *Biblical Critical Theory*, Zondervan Academic, 2023.

Watson David, *Discipleship*, Hodder and Stoughton, 1981.
    Is Anyone There? Hodder Christian Paperbacks, 1983.

Wells Samuel, *A Cross in the Heart of God*, Canterbury Press, 2020.

Williams Rowan, *The Way of St Benedict*, Bloomsbury Publishing, 2020.

BIBLICAL REFERENCES

Listed below are the Biblical texts I have referenced within each section of the book.

Introduction

Acts 7:54-58, John 10:10.

The Biblical Context of Discipleship

Acts 24:5, Mark 1:15, Matthew 13:44, Matthew 6:10, Matthew 5:3, Matthew 5:10, Matthew 28:19-20, 1 Corinthians 10:31, Exodus 33:11, Numbers 27, Deuteronomy 34, 1 Kings 19, 2 Kings 2, 2 Kings 2:3, 2 Kings 4:38, John 1:34, John 1:49, John 3:2, John 3:26, John 6:25, John 20:16, John 1:27, John 14:23, 1 Corinthians 11:1, John 15:8.

Step One – Sharing the Hope

1 Peter 3:15, John 3:16, Romans 3:23, Revelation 7:9, John 14:6, Acts 4:12, John 3:30, 2 Corinthians 12:9, 1 Timothy 2:4-6, Romans 10:9-13.

Step Two – Learning to Give

Luke 6:30, Luke 6:36, 1 John 4:8, Matthew 25:31-46, Acts 2:42-47, Proverbs 30:8-9.

Step Three – Growing in Prayer

Genesis 4:26, Exodus 2:23-24, Matthew 9:14, Matthew 6:8, Matthew 6:7, Matthew 6:5, Matthew 6:9-13, Luke 11:2-4, John 6:35.

Step Four – Willing to Forgive

Luke 7:36-50, John 8:2-11, Luke 23:34, Matthew 6:12, Matthew 5:38-39, Ephesians 4:32, James 5:15, John 15:1-17, 1 Corinthians 13, 1 John 2:3-11, 1 John 4:7-21, Matthew 18:15-18, 1 Corinthians 5, 2 Corinthians 2:5-11, Jonah 4.

Step Five – Willing to Go

John 15, Matthew 10:1-42, Matthew 10:6, Matthew 28:16-20, Acts 1:8, Genesis 12:1, Genesis 17:5, Exodus 2-3, Joshua 1, Jeremiah 1, Luke 8:38-39.

Step Six – Focussing on Worship

Genesis 22:5, John 4:24, Matthew 18:20, 1 Corinthians 14:26, Colossians 3:15-17, Philippians 2:5-11, Revelation 4:1-11, Revelation 7:9-17, Revelation 19:1-10.

Step Seven – Committing to Study

Proverbs 1:7, Proverbs 18:15, Matthew 11:29, John 14:15-17, Romans 15:4, Joshua 1:8, Proverbs 3:1, 2 Timothy 2:15, 2 Timothy 3:16, 2 Peter 1:20-21, 1 John 4:7-12, John 15:12-13, 1 Peter 4:8-9, 1 Corinthians 13, James 1:22.

Step Eight – Recognising your Gifts

1 Corinthians 12:8-10, Romans 12, Ephesians 4, 1 Corinthians 7:7, 1 Corinthians 13:3, 1 Corinthians 13, 1 Timothy 4:4, Galatians 5:22, Acts 2, Genesis 3, 1 Corinthians 12, 1 Corinthians 12:4, John 14:15- John 15:17.

Step Nine – Seeking the Kingdom

James 4:13-17, Luke 12:13-17, Romans 1:16, Philippians 2:5-11, Numbers 12:3, Revelation 21:1-5.

Step Ten – Keeping on Going

Luke 18:1-8, Matthew 24:1-35, Luke 11:5-8, Luke 9:51, Luke 22:39-46, James 5:11, Job 1:20-22, Job 2:7-10, Job 13:15.

BOOKS BY ALEX JACOB

"Receive The Truth" – sub titled "A collection of twenty questions and ten Bible talks focusing on key issues in contemporary Christian-Jewish relations and Christian spirituality".
ISBN: 9780 9567831-0-3, (Christian Publications International, 2011)

"The Case for Enlargement Theology" – *Second Edition.*
ISBN: 9780-9551790-8-2, (Christian Publications International, 2012)

"Prepare the Way" - sub-titled "A biblical exploration of four key advent themes: the Patriarchs, the Prophets, John the Baptist and Mary (the mother of Jesus), and how these themes prepare the way for the coming of Jesus",
ISBN: 9780-9926674-2-9 (Christian Publications International, 2014)

"Walking an Ancient Path" - sub-titled "Exploring four key New Testament Texts about Jesus".
ISBN: 9780-9926674-4-3, (Christian Publications International, 2016)

"100 Days With Luke" - sub-titled "Study Notes on the Gospel of Luke – an ideal resource for new Jewish believers in Jesus".
ISBN: 9780-9926674-8-1, (Christian Publications International, 2018)

"100 Days With Acts" - sub-titled "Study Notes on the Book of Acts – an ideal resource for new Jewish believers in Jesus".
ISBN: 9781-78926-508-8, (Christian Publications International, 2019)

"60 Days With Romans" - sub-titled "Study Notes on Paul's letter to the Romans – an ideal resource for new Jewish believers in Jesus".
ISBN: 9781-78926-516-3, (Christian Publications International, 2020)

CONTACT INFORMATION

If you would like to contact the author (Alex Jacob) with any questions or comments arising from this book please email Alex on revalexjacob@aol.com or stm@urceastern.org.uk. Your emails will be treated confidentially and Alex will try and respond directly by email.

www.ingramcontent.com/pod-product-compliance
Lightning Source LLC
Chambersburg PA
CBHW070315120526
44590CB00017B/2694